The Merchant of Venice

Artists: Penko Gelev

Sotir Gelev

Editor: Stephen Haynes
Editorial Assistants: Mark Williams, Tanya Kant

Published in Great Britain in MMX by
Book House, an imprint of
The Salariya Book Company Ltd
25 Marlborough Place, Brighton, BNI IUB
www.salariya.com
www.book-house.co.uk

ISBN-13: 978-1-906714-70-3 (PB)

SALARIYA

1 3 5 7 9 8 6 4 2

A CIP catalogue record for this book is available
from the British Library.

Printed and bound in China.
Printed on paper from sustainable sources.

Visit our website at **www.book-house.co.uk**
or go to **www.salariya.com**
for **free** electronic versions of:
You Wouldn't Want to be an Egyptian Mummy!
You Wouldn't Want to be a Roman Gladiator!
Avoid Joining Shackleton's Polar Expedition!
Avoid Sailing on a 19th-Century Whaling Ship!

Picture credits:
p. 40 Topfoto.co.uk
p. 47 ©KPA/TopFoto/TopFoto.co.uk Photographer: Honorar & Belege

Every effort has been made to trace copyright holders. The Salariya Book Company apologises for any omissions and would be pleased, in such cases, to add an acknowledgement in future editions.

The Merchant of Venice

William Shakespeare

Illustrated by

Penko Gelev

Retold by

Fiona Macdonald

Series created and designed by

David Salariya

The quality of mercy is not strained.
It droppeth as the gentle rain from heaven
Upon the place beneath. It is twice blest:
It blesseth him that gives and him that takes.

(See page 34)

CHARACTERS

Antonio, a merchant of
Venice, Italy

Bassanio, a nobleman,
cousin of Antonio

Shylock, a rich
Jewish banker

Portia, a rich
noblewoman

Gratiano, a friend of
Antonio and Bassanio

Salerio, a businessman

Solanio,
a businessman

Jessica, Shylock's
daughter

Lorenzo, a wild
young man

Nerissa, Portia's
servant

Launcelot Gobbo,
Shylock's servant

Tubal, a Jewish
banker, Shylock's
friend

Old Gobbo,
Launcelot's father

Duke of Venice,
ruler of the city

Prince of Morocco

Prince of Arragon

Two princes who both hope to marry Portia

ANTONIO'S SADNESS

Antonio the merchant is talking to his business friends, Salerio and Solanio.

In sooth[1] I know not why I am so sad.

Your mind is tossing on the ocean.[2]

Misfortune to my ventures,[3] out of doubt, would make *me* sad.

Believe me, no. My merchandise[4] makes me not sad.

They think that he must be worried about his trading ships, far away on dangerous voyages.

Why then, you are in love.

Fie, fie![5]

You look not well, Signor[6] Antonio.

Every man must play a part, and mine a sad one.

Antonio explains that he is not worried about business. He just feels doomed to lead a miserable life. Just then Bassanio, his best friend, arrives, with Gratiano and Lorenzo.

Let me play the fool. With mirth and laughter let old wrinkles[7] come.

Well, we will leave you then till dinner-time.

Gratiano speaks an infinite deal[8] of nothing.

Gratiano has different ideas. He wants a life full of fun. And he and Lorenzo are looking forward to their dinner!

At last, Antonio and Bassanio are alone. They can talk freely, without interruptions.

1. in sooth: truly.   2. Your mind is tossing on the ocean: You're worried about your ships and their valuable cargo.
3. ventures: business schemes.   4. merchandise: goods, trade.   5. Fie, fie!: Nonsense!   6. Signor: Italian for 'sir' or 'mister'.
7. old wrinkles: old age.   8. infinite deal: vast amount.

LOVE AND MONEY

Well, tell me now what lady is the same[1]...

...that you today promised to tell me of.

To you, Antonio, I owe the most in money and in love.

Antonio has an urgent question for his friend. Who is Bassanio in love with? At first Bassanio will not answer…

…but then he pours out his worries to Antonio. He has spent all his money, and borrowed lots more.

And from your love I have a warranty to unburthen all my plots and purposes[2] how to get clear of all the debts I owe.

My purse, my person, my extremest means[3] lie all unlocked to your occasions.[4]

Will Antonio, his best friend, help him repay his debts? Willingly, Antonio agrees.

In Belmont is a lady richly left[5] — and she is fair.[6]

All my fortunes are at sea.

To help Bassanio, he will have to borrow some.

Try what my credit can in Venice do.[7] Go presently inquire, and so will I.

Bassanio has lots more to say. He has met the woman he wants to marry – and to impress her he needs even more money! Antonio frowns. Just now, he has no cash to spare.

---

1. the same: the very one.   2. And from . . . purposes: Because you are such a good friend to me, it's only right that I should tell you all my schemes and plans.   3. extremest means: all that I have.   4. occasions: needs.   5. richly left: who has inherited a lot of money.   6. fair: beautiful.   7. Try . . . do: Find out how much money people in Venice are willing to lend me.

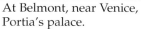

At Belmont, near Venice, Portia's palace.

Is it not hard?

But what warmth is there in your affection towards any of these princely suitors?[1]

First there is the Neapolitan[2] prince...

Portia, a rich heiress, complains to her trusted servant, Nerissa. It's not fair that she cannot choose her own husband.

Portia's father has died. He has chosen a very strange way to find a husband for her. Any man who wants to marry Portia must choose between three caskets. One of them contains a portrait of her. The man who chooses that one will marry her.

But Portia is not impressed by any of the men who have taken up the challenge.

From Scotland: too quarrelsome

From Naples: prefers horses

From France: too changeable

From England: speaks only English

I pray God grant them a fair departure!

From the Palatine (Germany): too gloomy

From Saxony (Germany): drinks too much

Do you not remember, lady? A Venetian, a scholar and a soldier?

Yes, yes, it was Bassanio. I remember him well.

The Prince of Morocco will be here tonight.

However, there is one handsome young man who has not yet taken the test.

But for the moment, there is another suitor who wishes to try Portia's marriage lottery.

1. suitors: men who want to marry.   2. Neapolitan: from Naples, in southern Italy.

9

SHYLOCK THE JEW

Venice: The Rialto Bridge, where merchants and bankers meet to do business

Three thousand ducats,[1] well.

Ay, sir, for three months.

Bassanio is trying to borrow money from Shylock, using Antonio's credit.[2]

Antonio is a good man. I think I may take his bond.[3]

Who is he who comes here?

This is Signor Antonio.

Shylock knows that Bassanio is poor. But he has heard good reports of Antonio.

I hate him for he is a Christian. He lends out money gratis[4] and brings down the rate of usance[5] here with us in Venice. Cursed be my tribe[6] if I forgive him.

Yet to supply the ripe[7] wants of my friend, I'll break a custom.

How much?

Antonio says that he never normally charges interest when he lends money, or pays it when he borrows. But for Bassanio's sake he'll make an exception.

If Shylock will lend money to Bassanio, Antonio will pay interest. What are Shylock's terms of business?

1. ducats: solid gold coins. 2. Antonio's credit: his reputation for being a trustworthy person to lend money to.
3. take his bond: accept his promise to pay back the money. A bond is a document recording a legal agreement.
4. gratis: free of charge. 5. usance: interest (extra money given to a lender by a borrower, when paying back a loan).
6. my tribe: According to the Bible, the ancient Israelites were divided into 12 tribes, each descended from Jacob; but here, Shylock may mean the Jewish people in general. 7. ripe: urgent.

You call me misbeliever, cut-throat dog, and spit upon my Jewish gaberdine.[1] Well then, it now appears you need my help.

If thou wilt[3] lend this money, lend it not as to thy[4] friends. Lend it rather to thine enemy.

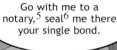

Hath[2] a dog money?

In the past, Antonio has insulted Jews. But he won't apologise. This is a business deal; he doesn't like Shylock, or care for his feelings.

Go with me to a notary,[5] seal[6] me there your single bond.

If you repay me not on such a day, let the forfeit[7] be...

...an equal pound of your fair flesh to be cut off.

Shylock says that he'll lend the money, if the deal can be legally recorded. Bassanio is very grateful.

Shylock does not want interest on his loan. Instead, he demands a shocking payment from Antonio.

Why, fear not, man: I will not forfeit it.[8] I do expect return[9] of thrice[10] three times the value of this bond.

O father Abraham, what these Christians are, whose own hard dealings teaches them suspect the thoughts of others!

The Hebrew[11] will turn Christian — he grows kind.

I like not fair terms and a villain's mind.[12]

Bassanio is horrified. Antonio tries to reassure him. Soon, his ships will come home, laden with treasure.

Scornfully, Shylock goes to consult his lawyers. Bassanio still does not trust him.

1. gaberdine: woollen cloak.　2. hath: has.　3. thou wilt: you will.　4. thy, thine: your.　5. notary: lawyer.
6. seal: mark with a seal (a blob of wax with a design stamped in it); a way of showing that a document was genuine.
7. forfeit: the penalty for not paying.　8. forfeit it: fail to pay back the loan.　9. return: profit on Antonio's trading voyages.
10. thrice: three times (so thrice three times = nine times as much).　11. Hebrew: Jew.　12. I like not . . . villain's mind: The agreement seems fair, but I still don't trust the man.

THE PRINCE OF MOROCCO

Portia's palace: The Prince of Morocco arrives.

Mislike me not for my complexion.[1] I would not change this hue,[2] except to steal your thoughts, my gentle queen.

The lottery of my destiny[3] bars me the right of voluntary choosing.

Portia is gracious, as always. She does not want to marry the Prince, but she has no choice – she must marry the man who chooses the right casket.

I pray you lead me to the caskets to try my fortune.

By this scimitar,[4] I would outbrave the heart most daring on the earth to win thee, lady.

You must take your chance.

After dinner your hazard shall be made.[5]

The Prince is keen to display his strength and courage, but Portia is not impressed.

The Prince wants to try the lottery as soon as possible.

1. complexion: skin colour; but at this period it can also mean 'character'.
2. hue: colour.   3. the lottery of my destiny: my fate, which will be decided by chance.   4. scimitar: sharp, curved sword.   5. your hazard shall be made: you shall try your luck.

Meanwhile, in a street near Shylock's house...

Do you not know me, Father?

It is a wise father that knows his own child.[1]

I am famished[2] in his service.

You may tell[3] every finger I have with my ribs.

Launcelot Gobbo, Shylock's servant, is looking for a new master. On the way, he meets an old, blind man.

He has heard that Bassanio is looking for servants.

Here comes the man. To him, father!

At Bassanio's house

I know thee well; thou has obtained thy suit.[4]

Yes, Launcelot can work for Bassanio if he wishes.

Signor Bassanio! I must go with you to Belmont.

Gratiano arrives. He has a favour to ask his friend.

Thou art too wild, too rude and bold of voice.

If I do not put on a sober habit[5]...

...never trust me more.

Bassanio is not certain. Will Gratiano's rowdy behaviour offend Lady Portia? Gratiano promises to be good – then goes to find his friends.

1. It is . . . child: Launcelot has muddled the well-known proverb 'It is a wise child that knows its own father.'
2. famished: starved.   3. tell: count. He means 'I am so thin that you can count my ribs with your fingers,' but he comically gets the words in the wrong order.   4. thy suit: the thing that you asked for (a job as Bassanio's servant).
5. put on a sober habit: behave like a serious, well-behaved person.

THE LOVERS' PLOT

Inside Shylock's house

Give him this letter; do it secretly.

I am sorry thou wilt[1] leave my father so.

Our house is hell, and thou, a merry devil, didst rob it of some taste of tediousness.[2]

Adieu![3] Most sweet Jew!

Jessica, Shylock's daughter, is saying goodbye to Launcelot.

Jessica hates her life as Shylock's daughter. She has fallen in love with Lorenzo, and is planning to run away with him.

What heinous[4] sin it is in me to be ashamed to be my father's child.

O Lorenzo! If thou keep promise, I shall end this strife,[5] become a Christian and thy loving wife.

Near Shylock's house. Lorenzo and his friends have a plan.

We will slink away in supper time, disguise us at my lodging, and return.

She hath directed[6] how I shall take her from her father's house.

Friend Launcelot, what's the news?

Launcelot delivers Jessica's letter to Lorenzo.

Jessica asks Lorenzo to come to Shylock's house in disguise, and help her escape – tonight!

1. thou wilt: you want to.   2. didst . . . tediousness: made it a bit less unpleasant.   3. adieu: goodbye for ever.
4. heinous: very terrible.   5. strife: trouble, quarrel (between Jessica and Shylock).   6. directed: sent instructions.

Shylock's house

Jessica! Jessica!

What is your will?

There are my keys.

Shylock is also preparing to leave home. He has been invited out to supper.

Shylock leaves Jessica in charge of his house while he is out for the evening.

There is some ill a-brewing...

What, are there masques?

Hear you me, Jessica: Lock up my doors.

But he is uneasy. He has had strange dreams, of money-bags. And he's heard that, tonight, there will masques[1] in the city.

Mistress, look out at window.

There will come a Christian by, Will be worth a Jewess' eye.

Launcelot whispers a secret message from Lorenzo.

What says that fool?

'Farewell, mistress' — nothing else.

Well, Jessica, go in. Do as I bid you.

Still suspicious, Shylock gets ready to meet his friends for dinner.

1. masques: performances with music, dancing, masks and elaborate disguises.

Escape by Night

Alone at last, Jessica must hurry.

Farewell.

And if my fortune be not crost,[1] I have a father, you a daughter, lost.

She rushes upstairs, to change into boy's clothes – and steal her father's treasure.

Meanwhile, Gratiano and Salerio wait impatiently in the street outside Shylock's house.

Are the friends in the right place?

His hour is almost past.[2]

This is the penthouse[3] under which Lorenzo desired us to make stand.

Sweet friends, your patience. Not I but my affairs[4] have made you wait.

Breathless, Lorenzo arrives. He is very sorry to be late.

Lorenzo! My love indeed!

Jessica, disguised as a boy, appears at an upstairs window.

Here, catch this casket.

1. crost: crossed; if my fortune be not crost: if all goes well.   2. His hour is almost past: He's nearly late.
3. penthouse: shelter with sloping roof.   4. affairs: business.

Descend!

Bravely, Jessica climbs down, to Lorenzo's waiting arms.

I love her heartily!

Wise, fair, and true, shall she be placed in my constant[1] soul.

Who's there?

On, gentlemen, away!

Now they must hurry, to escape from Venice before Shylock discovers that Jessica is missing and starts to search for her.

Lorenzo and Jessica have gone. As Gratiano walks home through the streets of Venice, he meets Antonio.

Where are all the rest? Bassanio presently will go aboard.

I am glad on't.[2]

Antonio has been looking for Gratiano and his friends. Bassanio's ship is ready to set sail for Belmont – and Portia.

1. constant: faithful, loving.   2. on't: about it.

Morocco Takes the Test

Belmont, Portia's palace. There are three caskets: gold, silver and lead.

Now make your choice.

How shall I know if I do choose the right?

Some god direct my judgement! Let me see...

The one of them contains my picture, prince. If you choose that, then I am yours withal.[1]

Portia explains the rules. The Prince must open one casket only. If he makes the wrong choice, he must never tell – and never marry!

Each casket has a riddle on it.

Gold... 'Who chooseth me shall gain what many men desire.'

Silver... 'Who chooseth me shall get as much as he deserves.'

Lead... 'Who chooseth me must give and hazard[2] all he hath.'

1. withal: also.   2. hazard: risk.

He has made his choice:

Here an angel
in a golden bed[1]
lies all within.

Deliver me the key.
Here do I choose.

The Prince decides to open the gold casket. That must be the right container for so precious a portrait.

Portia hands the key to the Prince. His choice will decide her future, as well as his own.

The Prince turns the key and lifts the lid.

Oh hell! What have we here?

'All that glisters[2]
is not gold;
Often have you
heard that told...'

Portia, adieu.
I have too grieved[3]
a heart to take a
tedious leave.[4]

A gentle riddance!

Morocco has made the wrong choice. He can never marry Portia, nor anyone else.

1. an angel in a golden bed: a beautiful portrait in a golden frame.   2. glisters: shines, glitters.
3. grieved: unhappy.   4. take a tedious leave: spend a long time saying goodbye politely.

My Daughter! My Ducats!

Venice: Salerio and Solanio are searching for Lorenzo.

Why, man, I saw Bassanio under sail.[1]

With him is Gratiano gone along — and in their ship I am sure Lorenzo is not.

The villain Jew with outcries[2] raised[3] the Duke.

In a gondola[4] were seen together Lorenzo and his amorous[5] Jessica.

Shylock's complaints are too late: Jessica and Lorenzo have escaped.

I never heard a passion[6] so confused, so strange...

My daughter! O my ducats! O my daughter!

Fled with a Christian!

Justice! The law! Find the girl!

1. under sail: on board a sailing ship.   2. outcries: shouts and complaints.   3. raised: alerted.
4. gondola: a special kind of rowing boat used only in Venice.   5. amorous: loving.   6. passion: fury.

Let good Antonio look he keep his day,[1] or he shall pay for this.

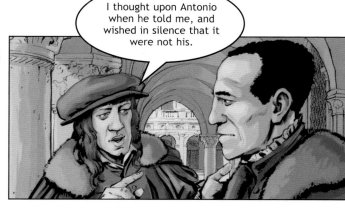

I thought upon Antonio when he told me, and wished in silence that it were not his.

Now Shylock is seeking revenge on all Christians. So Antonio is in danger! And there's worse news: a sailor reports that a rich Venetian ship has been wrecked. It might be one of Antonio's.

You were best to tell Antonio what you hear.

I saw Bassanio and Antonio part...

And for the Jew's bond...

...let it not enter in your mind.[2]

Be merry, and employ your chiefest thoughts[3] to courtship.

Antonio was sorry to see Bassanio leave. But bravely he hid his feelings, and did his best to encourage Bassanio.

Then Bassanio sailed away, to meet Portia in Belmont.

1. look he keep his day: be sure to repay his loan on time. 2. let it not enter your mind: forget all about it.
3. employ your chiefest thoughts: concentrate.

Arragon Makes his Choice

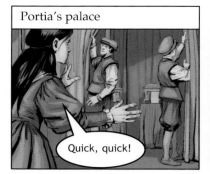

Portia's palace

Quick, quick!

Another suitor, the Prince of Arragon, has come to try the casket lottery.

Behold, there stand the caskets, noble prince!

Fortune now to my heart's hope![1]

Does the Prince dare? If he makes the wrong choice, he must never speak about it, and he must never marry.

Gold, silver and base[2] lead…

Ha, let me see…

He chooses the silver casket.

Give me a key for this, and instantly unlock my fortunes here.

'Who chooseth me shall get as much as he deserves.'

1. Fortune now to my heart's hope: Wish me luck!   2. base: worthless.

What's here? The portrait of a blinking idiot!

'There be fools alive, iwis!'[1]

But a clown's laughing face leers at him from the bottom of the casket.

Sweet, adieu. I'll keep my oath patiently to bear my wroth.[2]

Hanging and wiving goes by destiny.[3]

Portia is glad to see him go. She did not want to marry him. Nerissa quotes an old proverb.

Madam, there is alighted[4] at your gate a young Venetian — an ambassador of love.

Yet another visitor arrives at Portia's palace. Who can this be?

Come, come, Nerissa, for I long to see.

Bassanio, Lord Love,[5] if thy will it be!

1. iwis: indeed.   2. wroth: anger and disappointment.   3. Hanging and wiving goes by destiny: Death and marriage are decided by fate.   4. alighted: climbed down from a coach.   5. Lord Love: Cupid, the ancient Roman god of love. Nerissa is praying that the god of love will send Portia the suitor she wishes for.

Do We Not Bleed?

Back in Venice, the news is bad for Antonio.

Now what news?

Antonio hath a ship wracked.[1]

He hath lost a ship.

I would it might prove the end of his losses.[2]

How now, Shylock? What news among the merchants?

You knew of my daughter's flight.[3]

Shylock arrives. He is still furious, and still blames Antonio and his friends for Jessica's decision to run away with Lorenzo.

She is damned for it. My own flesh and blood to rebel!

Shylock is furious with Jessica, as well. He will never forgive her.

Do you hear whether Antonio have had any loss at sea?

The friends interrupt Shylock's angry ravings. They want more news of Antonio's ships.

1. wracked: wrecked.   2. I would it might prove the end of his losses: I hope he doesn't lose anything else. (The friends know that if Antonio cannot pay back the money, he may lose his life.)   3. flight: escape from Shylock's house.

Let him look to his bond.[1]

I am sure if he forfeit thou wilt not take his flesh.

What's that good for?

To bait fish.

Shylock is pleased to think that Antonio might be in trouble. In the past, Antonio was unkind to him; now it's Antonio's turn to suffer.

If all Antonio's ships are wrecked, he will have no money to repay Shylock. The bond demands a pound of his flesh, instead!

But Shylock wants the flesh.

He hath disgraced me, laughed at my losses, scorned my nation, thwarted my bargains[2]...

...cooled my friends, heated mine enemies.

It will feed my revenge.

Shylock has good reason to hate Antonio.

And Jewish people are human beings like anyone else. They have rights – and demand justice!

What's his reason? I am a Jew.

If you prick us, do we not bleed? And if you wrong us, shall we not revenge?

Hath not a Jew eyes? Hath not a Jew hands, senses, affections, passions?

1. look to his bond: remember his promise to repay the money or give up a pound of flesh.   2. thwarted my bargains: spoiled my business deals.

JESSICA'S TREACHERY

My master Antonio desires to speak with you both.

Here comes another of the tribe.[1]

A servant arrives with an urgent message for Salerio and Solanio. They leave – passing Tubal, Shylock's friend, who has just returned to Venice.

What news? Hast thou found my daughter?

I often came where I did hear of her.

The thief gone with so much — and no revenge!

Tubal has been searching for Jessica and Lorenzo, and for Shylock's missing treasure. Which does Shylock miss most – his daughter or his gold?

Other men have ill luck too. Antonio, as I heard, hath an argosy cast away.[2]

What, what, what? Ill luck? I thank God!

Tubal reports that another of Antonio's treasure-ships has been wrecked! Shylock is delighted.

Your daughter spent, one night, fourscore[3] ducats.

But his joy turns to horror when Tubal also tells him that Jessica has been seen spending money wildly.

1. another of the tribe: another Jewish person.   2. an argosy cast away: a treasure-ship lost.   3. fourscore: 80 (4 x 20).

I shall never see my gold again! Fourscore ducats at a sitting, fourscore ducats!

I am very glad of it. I'll plague him; I'll torture him.

Tubal has met merchants who say that Antonio will soon have lost all his money.

The same men have seen Jessica …

One of them showed me a ring that he had of[1] your daughter for a monkey.

I had it of Leah when I was a bachelor.

I would not have given it for a wilderness of monkeys.

Shylock is outraged – and heartbroken. The ring was his dear, dead wife's gift to him.

Antonio is certainly undone.[2]

Tubal tries to console Shylock.

Go, Tubal, fee me an officer.[3]

It's time to act! Shylock decides to have Antonio arrested for debt.

1. had of: obtained from.   2. undone: ruined.   3. fee me an officer: hire a policeman.

BASSANIO'S CHOICE

Bassanio has arrived at Belmont.

I would not[4] lose you.

I pray you tarry,[1] pause a day or two before you hazard,[2] for in choosing wrong[3] I lose your company.

He and Portia are very pleased to see each other. Romance is in the air…

Let me choose.

'Tell me where is fancy bred,[5] In the heart or in the head?'

If you do love me, you will find me out.

But Bassanio is desperate to marry Portia. He wants to try the casket lottery straight away.

Gaudy[6] gold, I will none of thee.[7] Nor none of thee, thou pale and common drudge.[8]

And here choose I. Joy be the consequence!

Oh love! I feel too much thy blessing!

Bassanio realises the caskets are a test of his character and intelligence. Will he judge them by their appearance, or think about what each metal means?

He chooses lead! It's plain and simple, honest and true.

Bassanio opens the casket…

1. tarry: wait.   2. hazard: risk the casket lottery.   3. in choosing wrong: if you choose the wrong casket.   4. would not: don't want to.   5. where is fancy bred: where does love come from? (but 'fancy' also means feelings, ideas, imagination).   6. gaudy: bright, showy.   7. I will none of thee: I don't want anything to do with you.   8. drudge: lowly servant. Bassanio calls silver a servant because it is used for everyday things such as coins.

...and finds Portia's portrait!

What find I here? Fair Portia's counterfeit![1]

'Turn to where your lady is And claim her with a loving kiss.'

This house, these servants, and this same myself are yours, my lord's.

...which when you part from, lose, or give away, let it presage[2] the ruin of your love.

When this ring parts from this finger, then parts life.

I give them with this ring...

Portia swears undying love to Bassanio, and gives him a ring. He must keep it, for ever!

Bassanio promises to wear the ring until the day he dies.

You saw the mistress, I beheld the maid. You loved, I loved.

Good joy, my lord and lady!

Meanwhile, Gratiano has asked Nerissa to marry him, and she has agreed. The happy couples congratulate each other.

1. counterfeit: copy, portrait.   2. presage: foretell, be a sign of.

29

More Trouble for Antonio

Salerio, Lorenzo and Jessica arrive at Portia's palace.

Welcome!

Signor Antonio commends him to you.[1]

Salerio hands Bassanio a letter. It's from Antonio.

Here are a few of the unpleasant'st[2] words that ever blotted paper!

But is it true? Hath all his ventures failed? What, not one hit?[3]

Bassanio reads the letter, and turns pale. Antonio is in terrible trouble.

Not one, my lord.

Salerio confirms the bad news. All Antonio's ships have sunk. Now he has no money…

Never did I know a creature so keen and greedy to confound[4] a man.

…and Shylock is demanding a pound of his flesh!

Pay him six thousand — double six thousand, and then treble that…

Portia wants to help. She is rich. She will pay any sum Shylock demands, and more.

First go with me to church and call me wife.[5]

Bassanio must go to Venice to help Antonio. But first, they will get married!

1. commends him to you: sends you his regards.   2. unpleasant'st: most unpleasant.   3. hit: success.
4. confound: harm, ruin.   5. call me wife: marry me.

Meanwhile, back in Venice...

Tell me not of mercy.

This is the fool that lent out money gratis.[1]

Antonio has been locked up in prison. Shylock mocks him, cruelly.

Hear me yet, good Shylock. I pray thee hear me speak.

Thou call'dst me[2] dog — beware my fangs. I'll have my bond!

I will have my bond.

Antonio begs Shylock to let him talk about ways of paying what he owes. But Shylock refuses.

Shylock storms out of the prison.

I am sure the Duke will never grant this forfeiture to hold.[3]

The Duke cannot deny the course of law. Pray God Bassanio come to see me pay his debt,[4] and then I care not.

Solanio tries to reassure Antonio. But Antonio cannot be comforted, and is very depressed.

1. gratis: for free, without charging interest.
2. Thou call'dst me: You used to call me.
3. grant this forfeiture to hold: allow this penalty to be paid.   4. pay his debt: have the pound of flesh cut from my body.

No Way Out!

Portia and Nerissa set off from Belmont, leaving Lorenzo and Jessica in charge.

> Madam, with all my heart, I shall obey you.

> See thou render[1] this into my cousin's hand.

Portia sends an urgent letter to her cousin, the famous lawyer Dr Bellario.

> Come on, Nerissa; I have work in hand that you yet[2] know not of.

Portia is planning a secret mission to save Antonio.

> How dost thou like the Lord Bassanio's wife?

> The world hath not her fellow.[3]

Venice: the law-court. The Duke[4] speaks to Antonio.

> I am sorry for thee. Thou art come to answer[5] an inhuman wretch, uncapable of pity.

> I am armed[6] to suffer with a quietness of spirit.

Antonio has now given up all hope of surviving. He waits calmly – but helplessly – for death.

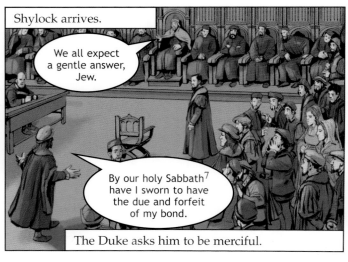

Shylock arrives.

> We all expect a gentle answer, Jew.

> By our holy Sabbath[7] have I sworn to have the due and forfeit of my bond.

The Duke asks him to be merciful.

1. render: deliver.   2. yet: so far.   3. not her fellow: no-one to equal her.   4. Duke: The ruler of Venice was called the Doge, which is the Venetian dialect word for 'duke'.   5. answer: defend yourself against.   6. armed: prepared.
7. Sabbath: Saturday, the Jewish holy day.

32

You'll ask me why I rather choose to have a weight of carrion[1] flesh

than to receive three thousand ducats.

I'll not answer that!

Thou unfeeling man!

Shylock still feels hurt by Antonio's past insults to his Jewish faith and traditions. In return, he wants to hurt Antonio.

I am not bound to please thee with my answers.

You may as well use question[2] with the wolf.

Make no more offers — let me have judgment, and the Jew his will.

Antonio is weak and depressed. He can stand no more arguments. He is willing to die.

But Bassanio will not give in.

For thy three thousand ducats here is six!

The pound of flesh — 'tis mine, and I will have it.

I stand for[3] judgment.

Answer: shall I have it?

I may dismiss this court unless Bellario — a learned doctor[4] whom I have sent for to determine this[5] — come here today.

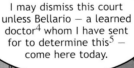

The Duke does not know what to do. He will wait until he has received advice from Dr Bellario — Portia's cousin.

1. carrion: dead.   2. use question: ask questions.
3. stand for: insist on.   4. doctor: expert lawyer.
5. determine this: solve this problem.

BALTHAZAR

Which is the merchant here, and which the Jew?

Do you confess the bond?

I do.

As the Duke speaks, Portia arrives in court, disguised as the lawyer Balthazar. No-one recognises her. Her mind is full of wise advice from top lawyer, Dr Bellario.

Then must the Jew be merciful.

The quality of mercy is not strained. It droppeth as the gentle rain from heaven. It blesseth him that gives and him that takes.[1]

I crave[2] the law, the penalty and forfeit of my bond.

Portia tries to make Shylock accept money instead of a pound of flesh cut from Antonio.

Shylock won't listen. He demands his rights – cruel though they are – according to the law.

Lawfully by this the Jew may claim a pound of flesh, to be by him cut off nearest the merchant's heart.

Be merciful, take thrice[3] thy money, bid me tear the bond.[4]

You must prepare your bosom[5] for his knife.

Portia demands to see the original agreement made between Shylock and Antonio. She reads it very carefully.

Once again, she asks Shylock to be merciful, and to take money instead of a pound of flesh. But he still wants revenge on Antonio – and on all other Christians who have mistreated him.

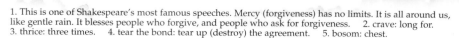

1. This is one of Shakespeare's most famous speeches. Mercy (forgiveness) has no limits. It is all around us, like gentle rain. It blesses people who forgive, and people who ask for forgiveness.   2. crave: long for.
3. thrice: three times.   4. tear the bond: tear up (destroy) the agreement.   5. bosom: chest.

O noble judge! O excellent young man!

Shylock is delighted.

The law allows no delay.

Are there balance[1] here to weigh the flesh?

I have them ready.

Have by some surgeon,[2] Shylock, to stop his wounds, lest he do[3] bleed to death.

Shylock says that providing medical care was not part of his original agreement with Antonio.

'Twere good you do so much for charity.[4]

'Tis not in the bond.

He wants to see Antonio suffer!

Give me your hand, Bassanio, fare you well.

Grieve not that I am fallen to this for you.[5]

I would lose all to deliver[6] you.

Antonio calls Bassanio, his best friend, to stand close beside him. He tells Bassanio not to blame himself for the suffering and death that he, Antonio, is about to endure.

A pound of that same merchant's flesh is thine. The court awards it, and the law doth give it.

Most rightful judge!

Tarry a little!

Take thou thy pound of flesh — but in the cutting it, if thou dost shed one drop of Christian blood,

thy lands and goods are, by the laws of Venice, confiscate[7] unto the state of Venice.

1. balance: scales. 2. Have by some surgeon: Have a doctor ready. 3. lest he do: so that he doesn't. 4. 'Twere good . . . for charity: It would be good if you did this out of kindness. 5. I am fallen to this for you: this has happened to me for your sake. 6. deliver: save. 7. confiscate: confiscated, taken away.

THE LAWYER'S FEE

Is that the law? I take this offer then. Pay the bond thrice and let the Christian go.

He shall have nothing but the penalty.

Shylock is horrified. How can he take flesh without taking blood? He now wants to accept the money instead.

Why, then the devil give him good of it![1] I'll stay no longer question.[2]

Tarry, Jew! The law hath yet another hold on you.

But Portia will not change her legal opinion. Shylock must have the pound of flesh – or nothing!

Half thy wealth, it is Antonio's. The other half comes to the general state.[4]

Thou hast not left the value of a cord![3]

Gratiano taunts Shylock.

Because Shylock has tried to harm a Venetian citizen (Antonio), he must be punished. He is to lose all his money.

Antonio does not want Shylock's money. Instead, he asks him to become a Christian – and leave all he owns to Lorenzo and Jessica.

What dost thou say?

I am content.

Sir, I entreat[5] you home with me to dinner.

I must away this night.

The Duke congratulates Portia.

We stand indebted

in love and service to you evermore.

Most worthy gentleman!

He is well paid that is well satisfied.

Antonio and Bassanio thank the young lawyer. Portia says she is pleased to have been able to help them, and does not want to be paid for her services.

1. the devil give him good of it: it's cursed; he can keep it!   2. I'll stay no longer question: I won't argue any longer.
3. Thou hast . . . cord: You can't even afford a rope to hang yourself.   4. the general state: the city of Venice.
5. entreat: invite.

Will she at least accept a gift to remember them by?

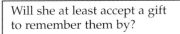

Take some remembrance of us as a tribute.

I'll take this ring.

Good sir, this ring was given me by my wife.

Portia sees the ring on Bassanio's hand. But Bassanio does not want to give it to her!

She made me vow[1] that I should neither sell nor give nor lose it.

She would not hold out enemy[2] for ever.

Well, peace be with you!

My Lord Bassanio, let him have the ring.

Go, Gratiano, give him the ring.

Portia tries to persuade Bassanio. Surely, his wife would forgive him? Bassanio disagrees.

It's time for Portia to leave. Bassanio still has not recognised her. She must get back to Belmont before he does.

Bassanio thinks again.

A street near the law-court

My Lord Bassanio, upon more advice[3] hath sent you here this ring.

His ring I do accept most thankfully.

Sir, I would speak with you.

I'll see if *I* can get *my* husband's ring.

With mixed feelings, Portia accepts the ring. Has Bassanio already forgotten his wedding-day promise to her?

Nerissa decides to try to get back the ring she gave Gratiano. She also needs his help, to collect something from Shylock.

1. vow: solemnly promise.   2. hold out enemy: continue to be angry with you.
3. upon more advice: after thinking about it.

HAPPY EVER AFTER

Here will we sit and let the sounds of music creep in our ears.

That night, Lorenzo and Jessica walk in the gardens of Portia's palace.

That light we see is burning in my hall. How far that little candle throws his beams!

Portia and Nerissa approach the palace. They have changed out of their lawyers' disguise into women's clothes.

Music! Hark!

Dear lady, welcome home.

We have been praying for our husbands' welfare.[1]

Are they returned?

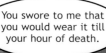

Your husband is at hand.[2]

Lorenzo greets them. But where are Bassanio and Gratiano? Have they returned from the law-court in Venice?

You are welcome home, my lord.

This is Antonio, to whom I am so infinitely bound.[3]

Bassanio introduces his dear old friend, Antonio, to Portia.

But suddenly Nerissa and Gratiano start quarrelling.

You swore to me that you would wear it till your hour of death.

My lord Bassanio gave *his* ring away...

What ring?

Not that, I hope, which you received of me?

Portia hears Gratiano saying that Bassanio gave his ring away. Quickly, she questions her husband.

38   1. praying for our husbands' welfare: praying that they are well.   2. at hand: near.
3. infinitely bound: eternally grateful.

By my honour, madam! No woman had it, but a civil doctor.[1]

I was enforced to send it after him.

I was beset with shame and courtesy.[2]

Bassanio and Gratiano both try to explain. Bassanio says that he had no choice. He had to give the ring to the lawyer who saved Antonio's life.

I'll have that doctor for my bedfellow.

And I his clerk.[3]

Portia and Nerissa tease their husbands.

Portia, forgive me.

Bassanio is very, very sorry.

Your lord will never more break faith.

Antonio promises that he will make sure Bassanio behaves well in future.

Give him this, and bid him[4] keep it better than the other.

Portia was the doctor, Nerissa there her clerk.

To Bassanio's amazement, Portia produces the missing ring, and admits that she was the lawyer, in disguise.

Bassanio and Gratiano are astonished – and relieved.

Were you the clerk?

Were you the doctor and I knew you not?

My ships are safely come to road.[5]

Meanwhile, Antonio has received an urgent letter. It contains wonderful news: his ships are safe! He is rich once more.

Nerissa hands over the agreement that she went to collect from Shylock. When he dies, Jessica and Lorenzo will have all his money!

The end

1. a civil doctor: a doctor of civil law; an expert on the kind of law that has to do with contracts and disputes, rather than crime.   2. beset with shame and courstesy: overpowered by feelings of shame and good manners.   3. clerk: lawyer's assistant.   4. bid him: tell him to.   5. road: entrance to a harbour.

WILLIAM SHAKESPEARE (1564–1616)

William Shakespeare lived over 400 years ago. Yet today, his plays are still performed worldwide, on stage and on TV, in films, and as operas, ballets and musicals. He is probably the most famous playwright who has ever lived – and yet very little is known about his private life or his individual personality. No documents written by him have survived, apart from his will and a few legal papers, and there are no surviving descriptions written by people who knew him. The only clues we have to Shakespeare's thoughts and feelings are hidden in his poetry and plays.

SHAKESPEARE'S YOUTH

Shakespeare was born in Stratford-upon-Avon, a market town in the English Midlands, on 23 April 1564. He came from one of Stratford's top families. Although his grandparents had been poor, ordinary farmers, his father, John Shakespeare, had moved into Stratford town, where he worked as a glove-maker and wool-trader. He grew rich, and was chosen by other businessmen to be Stratford's mayor.

Almost certainly, John Shakespeare had enough money to send his son to the local grammar school. There, young William would have learned to read and write: certainly in English, probably in Latin and perhaps in Greek. He would have been taught many stories about Ancient Greece and Rome, and would also have studied the Bible. Unlike boys from richer or more noble families, Shakespeare did not go to university. This makes his writings –

Portrait of Shakespeare by Martin Droeshout, on the title-page of the First Folio edition of Shakespeare's plays (London, 1623)

which feature brilliant, beautiful language, clever, complicated plots, wide knowledge of history, and deep insight into human character and behaviour – all the more remarkable.

FAMILY MAN

William Shakespeare probably left school some time around 1580, when he would have been 16 years old. Just two years later, aged 18, he married Anne Hathaway, a local farmer's daughter. She was eight years older than him, and pregnant with their first child. It was a daughter, named Susanna; in 1585, Anne had twins – a daughter, Judith, and a son, Hamnet. Like many other Tudor children, Hamnet died from an infection, when he was only 11 years old.

The 'lost years'

Soon after the twins were born, Shakespeare left Stratford. No-one today knows where he went to or what he was doing for the next six years. Some historians think that he may have worked as a schoolmaster in a rich family's stately home in Lancashire, in northern England. Others suggest that he became a soldier and travelled abroad, fighting in Europe. Certainly, Shakespeare's writings tell us that he knew many words in foreign languages. And several of his plays, including *The Merchant of Venice*, are set in Italy.

Shakespeare and the theatre

In 1592, a booklet of jokes, published in London, tells us that Shakespeare was living there. Now aged 28, he was working as an actor, and also writing plays. We don't know how he began this career; probably he joined a troop of touring actors who travelled around England, or perhaps he made friends with one of the many playwrights working in London at that time. Famous, fashionable, writers included Christopher Marlowe, Thomas Nashe, Thomas Middleton and John Fletcher. Later in his career, Shakespeare wrote plays together with many of them.

However he got started, Shakespeare soon became a great success. By 1594, he is listed as a 'sharer' (investor and part owner) of a new theatre company, The Lord Chamberlain's Men. In 1599, he also invested in London's newest and greatest theatre, the Globe. He used other money made from his plays to buy a splendid family home back in Stratford-upon-Avon: New Place, the second-largest house in town.

Later life

In 1614, Shakespeare gave up acting and writing after completing about 40 plays. He left London, and returned to Stratford where his wife and daughters were living. But sadly he was not able to enjoy his retirement for long.

Shakespeare's memorial

William Shakespeare died in 1616, aged only 52. His body was buried in Holy Trinity churchyard in Stratford. His tombstone was carved – not with his own great poetry, but with the following simple verse:

'Blessed be the man that spares
  these stones,
And cursed be he that moves
  my bones.'

Shakespeare's Theatre

The first permanent theatre in London was opened in 1576 in Shoreditch, to the north of the city. It was called The Theatre, from an ancient Greek word which means 'a place for seeing things'. Before this time, companies of actors travelled around the country, performing in inn yards and public squares.

The first 'playhouses' of Shakespeare's time were roughly circular, three-storey buildings. There was a ring-shaped thatched roof over the three tiers of seats, but the central part was open to the sky. It cost a penny to stand in the central pit, and twopence or more for a seat in one of the galleries. Audiences were very tightly packed, and whenever the plague came to London the theatres were closed to prevent the spread of infection.

Performances were held in the afternoons. There was no interval, but you could buy snacks during the play. The play was usually followed by a comic sketch with singing and dancing, which was called a 'jig'.

The Globe
The most famous theatre that Shakespeare's company performed in was The Globe. It was on Bankside, south of the Thames. The Globe was built in 1599 from the timbers of the old Theatre in Shoreditch. When the lease for the old building ran out, the actors dismantled the theatre during the night and moved it across the river.

The Globe burned down in 1613 during a performance of *Henry VIII*, when a spark from a cannon on stage set light to the thatched roof.

Elizabethan plays
Elizabethan audiences loved excitement and spectacle: they wanted to be entertained, and they liked variety. Theatre managers had to keep them happy, as Shakespeare was very well aware. This meant that theatres needed a constant supply of new plays and new writers. Often, several writers worked together on one play, each writing the bits they were good at.

The main types of play were tragedies, about the downfall of heroic men, and comedies, which were lighthearted and ended happily ever after, but weren't necessarily funny. There were also pastoral plays, about shepherds and simple country life, and historical plays, which reminded people about the great heroes of the past, particularly English kings. Shakespeare could turn his hand to any of these, and some of his plays combine elements of several styles.

Boy actors
Whatever the plot, all the women's parts – even beautiful Portia's – were played by boys whose voices had not yet broken. Women were not allowed to perform in public. Most Elizabethans thought that actors were 'low-life' and possibly even criminal. Certainly, the rowdy crowds that flocked to their plays often included pickpockets and thieves.

FEAR OF FOREIGNERS

Shakespeare has often been criticised for the anti-Semitic (anti-Jewish) opinions that he gives to some of his characters in *The Merchant of Venice*. Antonio, in particular, while loyal and kind to his Christian friends, is shockingly rude and hurtful to Shylock and other Jews. He spits on Shylock, kicks him, and calls him a 'dog'. Shakespeare's play contains many other examples of anti-Jewish words and actions that we find extremely offensive – and unlawful – today, including Shylock's forced conversion to Christianity at the end of his trial. This racial and cultural prejudice extends to all foreigners in the play. Even wise Portia clearly dislikes all the foreign suitors who come to her palace.

Why did Shakespeare include such hateful insults and opinions? Firstly, because he wanted to explore the ways in which people from different traditions fail to understand each other, even though we are all members of the same human race. As Shylock says, in one of Shakespeare's most famous pieces of writing: 'If you prick us, do we not bleed?' He means that in spite of outward differences, we are really all the same.

Secondly, Shakespeare wanted to make us think deeply about whether revenge – as demanded by Shylock – can ever be justified. And he shows how cruelty and insults (for example, from Antonio) can create hatred and a wish to harm in victims (such as Shylock).

Thirdly, Shakespeare was reflecting popular opinions at the time he lived. In the sixteenth century, Europe was much less multicultural than it is today. Almost everyone was deeply suspicious of strangers – people who looked, sounded or behaved differently from themselves. In England, for example, Jewish people were not allowed to live or worship freely. They did not have the same legal rights as the majority Christian community. Often, they had to hide their identity and pretend to be Christians, in order to live peacefully alongside their neighbours.

JEWS IN VENICE

In real-life Venice, Jewish people had to live shut away in just one part of the city, which was called the Ghetto. Since then, the word 'ghetto' has come to mean any place in which members of a deprived minority group live. Venetian Jews had to wear red or yellow hats so that they could easily be recognised.

POLITICS AND RELIGION

For much of Shakespeare's lifetime, England was at war, or feared invasion by foreign armies. English traders and explorers faced fierce competition from rival foreign merchants, at home and overseas. Everywhere in Europe, citizens guarded their privileges, such as the right to set up shops or own property, and denied these rights to anyone born outside their city's walls. Then – just like today – politics often mixed with religion, with deadly conquences. Fearing rebellion – and wanting an entirely Christian kingdom – the rulers of Spain expelled all Jews and Muslims in 1492. In eastern Europe, too, there were many bitter battles between Christians and Muslims.

Love and Money

The plot of *The Merchant of Venice* is based on key human concerns: hatred and prejudice, friendship and loyalty, love and money. Throughout the play, the last two are very closely connected. Shakespeare often uses just one word, 'fortunate' (meaning 'rich' or 'happy and lucky'), to describe them both. Out of love for his friend Bassanio, Antonio borrows money from Shylock; to elope with Lorenzo, Jessica steals and sells treasures; Bassanio hopes to become 'fortunate' by marrying Portia.

Is Shakespeare sending a message by these storylines, that 'money can buy happiness'? Perhaps so. Certainly, at the time when Shakespeare lived, no-one believed that 'all you need is love'. Among wealthy families, marriage was normally a matter of business; marriages were arranged by parents for their children. Only older people, like Nerissa and Gratiano (whose parents are dead), had the freedom to find a partner for themselves.

Marriage was an important way of making links between families, and of transferring wealth and land. Girls had to bring a dowry (a gift of cash or property) to their new husband; once married, all a woman's possessions passed to her husband. That is one of the reasons why so many men are keen to marry Portia. By wedding her, they win not only a wise and beautiful woman, but enormous wealth.

When arranging marriages, most parents took care to choose a partner of good character for their son or daughter. In *The Merchant of Venice*, Jessica's elopement is shocking for Lorenzo's family as well as for Shylock. Daughters, including Jessica, were meant to be modest and obedient and not leave home without permission; running away with a man was scandalous. Sons, including Lorenzo, brought shame on their family by marrying women who did disgraceful things like dressing in men's clothes – and stealing money and jewels. Both Christian and Jewish parents disapproved of their children marrying into different religious traditions.

PORTIA'S LOTTERY

In *The Merchant of Venice*, the wedding lottery arranged by Portia's father is a test of courage, commitment and character for the men who dare to try it – though it gives Portia no choice. It seems strange to us today, and was unusual even in Shakespeare's time. It was, however, a well-known topic in stories. When Shakespeare borrowed it to use in his play, he was blending real life with fantasy.

LENDING MONEY

In Shakespeare's time, the Christian Church forbade people who loaned money to collect interest (extra payments) on it. So did many state governments, although English laws did allow lenders to charge low borrowing fees. In contrast, Jewish holy laws did not ban any kind of interest charges. That is why most bankers and money-lenders in Shakespeare's Europe were Jewish. They provided very useful services, lending money or keeping it safe, for businesses of all kinds.

TIMELINE OF EVENTS

1558
Elizabeth I, daughter of Henry VIII, becomes Queen of England.

1564
William Shakespeare is born on 23 April in Stratford-upon-Avon, Warwickshire.

1568
Shakespeare's father becomes Bailiff (mayor) of Stratford-upon-Avon.

1570
Shakespeare's father is fined (twice) for charging too much interest on loans.

1572
Parliament passes a law regarding the punishment of vagrants (tramps), including travelling actors.

1576
The Theatre, the first permanent playhouse in London, is built in Shoreditch, on the north side of the river Thames.

1582
Shakespeare marries Anne Hathaway.

1583
Shakespeare's daughter Susanna is born.

1585
Birth of Shakespeare's twins, Hamnet and Judith.

1587
Five troupes of touring actors visit Stratford; possibly Shakespeare joins one of them. The play *Tamburlaine the Great* by star playwright Christopher Marlowe is first performed in London, and is a great success.

1588
The Spanish Armada is defeated and England is saved from invasion.

1592
An outbreak of plague closes the playhouses; instead of plays, Shakespeare writes poems and sonnets.

1593
Shakespeare's most famous rival playwright, Christopher Marlowe, is killed in a tavern fight, aged 29.

1594
The playhouses reopen. Shakespeare joins the Lord Chamberlain's Men as actor and playwright.

1596
Shakespeare's son Hamnet dies, aged 11.

1597
Shakespeare buys New Place, the second-biggest house in Stratford.

1599
The Globe opens on Bankside. Shakespeare is a 'sharer' or stockholder. He writes several of his most important plays around this time.

1603
Queen Elizabeth dies without an heir. James VI of Scotland becomes King of England, taking the title James I. The Lord Chamberlain's Men troupe of players is reorganised as the King's Men.

1605
The Gunpowder Plot, a conspiracy to assassinate James I and his Parliament, is foiled on 5 November.

1608–1609
New, indoor theatres begin to be built in London.

1613
Shakespeare's Globe is destroyed by fire but rebuilt the following year.

1616
William Shakespeare dies in Stratford on 23 April.

1623
Two of Shakespeare's former theatrical colleagues publish the First Folio, a collected edition of his dramatic works.

PLAYS BY WILLIAM SHAKESPEARE

Note: We do not know the precise dates when most of Shakespeare's plays were written or first performed, or the exact order in which they were written. The dates shown here are only approximate.

1590–1591:	*Two Gentlemen of Verona*
	The Taming of the Shrew
1591:	*Henry VI, Part II*
	Henry VI, Part III
1592:	*Henry VI, Part I**
	*Titus Andronicus**
1594:	*The Comedy of Errors*
	Edward III (?)
1594–1595:	*Love's Labours Lost*
1595:	*Richard II*
	Romeo and Juliet
	A Midsummer Night's Dream
1596:	*King John*
1596–1597:	*The Merchant of Venice*
	Henry IV, Part I
1597–1598:	*The Merry Wives of Windsor*
	Henry IV, Part II
1598:	*Much Ado About Nothing*
1598–1599:	*Henry V*
1599:	*Julius Caesar*
1599–1600:	*As You Like It*
1600–1601:	*Hamlet*

1600–1601:	*Twelfth Night*
1602:	*Troilus and Cressida*
1603:	*Measure for Measure*
1603–1604:	*Sir Thomas More**
	Othello
1604–1605:	*All's Well that Ends Well*
1605:	*Timon of Athens**
1605–1606:	*King Lear*
1606:	*Macbeth*
	Anthony and Cleopatra
1607:	*Pericles**
1608:	*Coriolanus*
1609:	*The Winter's Tale*
1610:	*Cymbeline*
1611:	*The Tempest*
1613:	*Henry VIII*
	*Cardenio** (lost)
1613–1614:	*Two Noble Kinsmen**

* = written jointly with other playwrights
(?) = perhaps not by Shakespeare

DO YOU SPEAK SHAKESPEARE?

Shakespeare's writing is so powerful that many lines from his poems and plays have become part of everyday English language. Many books, songs and films also use Shakespeare's words for their titles.

Perhaps you use some of his words and phrases yourself, or have heard people speaking them in films or on the radio and TV? Here are a few of the best-known:

'You and yours'
'To be or not to be?'
'A tower of strength'
'All the world's a stage.'
'Green-eyed jealousy'
'The sound(s) of music'
'At one fell swoop'
'A fool's paradise'
'A sea-change'
'A sorry sight'
'All that glisters is not gold.'

PERFORMING *THE MERCHANT*

The Merchant of Venice is a shocking play. Some actors are unwilling to speak Shakespeare's words, and audiences are often uncomfortable when listening to them. Unlike many Shakespeare plays, it has not proved popular with film-makers.

Several short scenes from *The Merchant* were filmed in the early 20th century, and silent movies based on the play were made in France and Germany in 1910 and 1923. But it was not until 2004 that a full-length feature film, with sound, was produced in English. It starred Hollywood leading man Al Pacino as Shylock.

Filmed versions of stage performances have also appeared, including one in 1973 with famous British actor Laurence Olivier as Shylock. Other versions have been specially made for TV. In New Zealand, an adaptation of the story, translated into the Maori language, was filmed in 2002.

Directors and producers have often felt the need to change Shakespeare's text of *The Merchant*, censor offensive scenes or suggest alternative endings. Casting and performing choices have also shaped its meaning. For example, in the USA in 1994, all Jewish parts in the play were taken by Black actors, to highlight its racist content. One TV movie of *The Merchant*, made in 2001, was set in pre-Holocaust Nazi Germany. In 1976, British playwright Arnold Wesker felt so outraged by Shakespeare's original story that he wrote a whole new version showing Antonio and Shylock as good friends.

Al Pacino (right) as Shylock in the 2004 film directed by Michael Radford

INDEX

If you liked this book, you might like to try these other Graffex titles:

Adventures of Huckleberry Finn Mark Twain

Dr Jekyll and Mr Hyde
  Robert Louis Stevenson

Dracula Bram Stoker

Frankenstein Mary Shelley

Hamlet William Shakespeare

The Hunchback of Notre Dame Victor Hugo

Jane Eyre Charlotte Brontë

Journey to the Centre of the Earth Jules Verne

Julius Caesar William Shakespeare

Kidnapped Robert Louis Stevenson

The Last of the Mohicans
  James Fenimore Cooper

Macbeth William Shakespeare

The Man in the Iron Mask Alexandre Dumas

Moby-Dick Herman Melville

The Odyssey Homer

Oliver Twist Charles Dickens

Romeo and Juliet William Shakespeare

A Tale of Two Cities Charles Dickens

The Three Musketeers Alexandre Dumas

Treasure Island Robert Louis Stevenson

Twenty Thousand Leagues Under the Sea
  Jules Verne

Wuthering Heights Emily Brontë